Original title:

The Greenest Room

Copyright © 2025 Creative Arts Management OÜ
All rights reserved.

Author: Adrian Caldwell
ISBN HARDBACK: 978-1-80581-724-6
ISBN PAPERBACK: 978-1-80581-251-7
ISBN EBOOK: 978-1-80581-724-6

Sanctuary of Sunlight

In a room where laughter grows,
Sunbeams tickle toes.
Houseplants throw a wacky dance,
Even cacti join the chance.

Leaves whisper silly tunes,
Bouncing like cheerful loons.
The sun hangs low and wide,
As squirrels take a joyful ride.

Flourishing Retreat

A cozy nook with a quirky twist,
Where herbs and jokes coexist.
Chives chuckle with delight,
As basil wears a hat so bright.

Lettuce plays hide and seek,
With peppers making squeaky squeaks.
In this vibrant, leafy zone,
Every corner feels like home.

Tranquil Haven

In shadows where the greens convene,
Ferns dance like a wacky machine.
Pothos tells a pun or two,
While succulents plot to make stew.

Cushions, plump with giggles rife,
Serve as seats for the plant life.
A hammock sways, oh what a show,
As vines wrap around like a pro!

Where Vines Embrace

A place where vines like to play,
Swinging gently every day.
Laughter echoes in the air,
As ferns steal the spotlight with flair.

Moss joins in to roll on the floor,
While ivy tells jokes galore.
In this leafy, lively space,
Even silence wears a face!

Sustenance in Nature's Art

In the jungle where bananas grow,
Monkeys dance, putting on a show.
Their smiles wide, oh what a sight,
Chasing coconuts with all their might.

Lemons roll like little suns,
While papayas hide, just for fun.
Watermelons wear silly hats,
As squirrels gossip, chitchat with bats.

Mango tango on the vine,
Strawberries sing to the twinkling pine.
Each berry a jester in nature's court,
Adding laughter, they play and cavort.

So laugh with me and take a bite,
In this feast, everything feels right.
Nature's art, so bright and bold,
A banquet of giggles, stories told.

Treetops' Tender Twilight

Beneath the stars, where treetops sway,
Owls crack jokes at the end of day.
Squirrels wear capes, flying around,
While crickets play the nighttime sound.

The moon, a playful little child,
Peeks through leaves, so sweet and mild.
As shadows dance on the forest floor,
Even the mushrooms giggle and snore.

Fireflies flicker, a circus act,
Illuminating secrets, no need to pact.
Raccoons in masks, plotting their schemes,
Hatching plans for stealing dreams.

So join the party, let's all cheer,
In nature's realm, there's nothing to fear.
With friends so silly, both near and far,
The twilight's magic is what we are.

Resplendent Breathing Spaces

In a room filled with leaves, oh what a sight!
Socks with plants dance, under the moonlight.
Lurking in shadows, a frog starts to croak,
Quipping to curtains, the shy little bloke.

Moss pillows gather dust, with stories untold,
Ferns gossip softly, as they share tales of old.
A spotted cat naps on a vine-draped chair,
Dreaming of mice that float in the air.

Harmonies of the Herbarium

Amidst greenery lush, the plants hold a feast,
Basil's rapping beats, while dill's quite the beast.
Sage sings a ballad, thyme joins in the fun,
Under a jolly sun, their concert's begun!

Cacti in the corner roll their prickly eyes,
As petunias sway, bringing vibrant surprise.
A spider, a DJ, spins webs made of sound,
While ivy grows wild, dancing round and round.

Footsteps on Mossy Floors

In this place where the mushrooms grow tall and round,
Every shuffle and giggle echoes the sound.
A worm in a wig, struts proudly on stage,
Reciting sweet sonnets, while turning the page.

The floor is a carpet, of soft moss and cheer,
As puddles reflect, the laughter we hear.
A snail with a shell that looks just like cheese,
Says life's but a joke, take it lightly, if you please!

Dialogue of Thorns and Blossoms

In a chat between roses, and thorns armed with glee,
The joke's on the gardener, can't you see?
'Why are we pruned?' boasts a vibrant tulip,
'It's for your own good!' quips a stubborn lilac.

The daisies hold court, all fluffy and bright,
While violets complain they don't get enough light.
They giggle and bicker, a playful bouquet,
In a fragrant debate that brightens the day.

Retreat Among the Foliage

In a space where leaf piles play,
The squirrels hold a grand café.
Moss tickles toes like gentle jest,
And sunlight beams, a furry guest.

Ferns dance whimsically in glee,
Chasing shadows like a spree.
A chubby hedgehog leads the way,
With a disco ball made of hay.

The butterflies start a live band,
On petals they frolic and stand.
Laughter erupts with every flap,
As ants serve snacks at the picnic map.

Green confetti falls from above,
In a forest party, full of love.
We toast with twigs, raise a cheer,
For the wildest retreat, have no fear!

The Call of the Wild Boughs

Branches beckon with leafy grins,
As bushes share their merry sins.
A raccoon does the limbo dance,
While rabbits giggle, lost in chance.

In this realm of vibrant trance,
Flowers pull off a wiggly prance.
Laughter echoes off the bark,
As critters swap their wild remark.

The trees wear hats of vibrant green,
In a carnival, we've never seen.
An owl DJ spins the tunes,
As frogs croak notes to the moons.

The boughs will call, they sing so clear,
Join in their mirth, forget your fear.
When life feels dull, just follow their song,
In the wild, the laughers belong!

Opus of the Emerald

Lush tunes echo through the vale,
As nature's band begins to sail.
With frogs on drums and bees on lute,
They strike a chord none can dispute.

Leaves shimmy to their rhythm bright,
Grasses sway in sheer delight.
A cheerful gnome conducts the show,
With a wink and nod to all below.

Tulips twirl in a funny way,
As daisies giggle, bluebirds play.
A symphony of joy unfolds,
In the green where the laughter molds.

So sit awhile and hear the sound,
Of jolly antics all around.
Let the opus of the emerald ring,
In the heart of nature, let's all sing!

Calm in Color's Embrace

In hues of nature, laughter lies,
Where wiggly vines are the best surprise.
Pineapples wear a crown so neat,
And carrots hop on little feet.

Sunflowers pull a silly face,
While mushrooms host a dance-off race.
With every breeze, a chuckle's found,
Tickling leaves with a bright, soft sound.

The whispering grass joins in the fun,
Tickling toes 'til the day is done.
In this embrace of color so bold,
Even the shyest souls break the mold.

So let's bask in this playful cheer,
In nature's arms, there's nothing to fear.
With laughter topping the leafy scene,
In this joyful oasis, we glean!

Haven of the Heart's Bloom

In a cozy nook with a plant that spins,
Laughter erupts where the mischief begins.
Dwarfs with a grin on a shelf full of cheer,
Plotting and scheming to make joy a sphere.

With plush little cushions that bounce off the walls,
A cactus named Spike who insists on his calls.
He tells all the jokes, though they prick a bit tight,
We laugh even louder in the soft morning light.

Glades of Serenity

In a room full of vines where the sunlight breaks,
Charming little dragons make funny mistakes.
They trip over leaves and slide on the floor,
Chasing each other, they burst through the door.

A fern wears a hat that's too big for its head,
While a flower sings loudly, ignoring its bed.
The moments are silly, yet peaceful they seem,
In this sanctuary, we tumble and dream.

Tending to the Untamed

With hands in the dirt, the day starts with fun,
We talk to the weeds, as if they could run.
A gnome on a stake gives a wink and a nod,
"Pull 'em right out, or they'll make quite the plod!"

The fruit trees are grumbling, they want to be fed,
While squirrels hold a meeting on tops of my shed.
Each morning is chaos, and yet, so divine,
This wild little garden, a place that's all mine.

Life Among the Foliage

In a jungle of green where the laughter is strong,
The laughter of crickets joins in with the throng.
A snail's got a race against time, oh so slow,
Calls out to the flowers, "Well, come on, let's go!"

The blooms wear their colors like a silly disguise,
They tease each other with the brightest of lies.
With every warm breeze, they shake up their roots,
Life's a grand party, in gardening boots.

Hushed Conversations with Ferns

In the corner, ferns do peek,
Whispering secrets, so to speak.
They giggle, wiggling in delight,
As sunlight dances, oh what a sight.

They gossip low, about the pines,
Who drapes themselves in shady lines.
"Did you see the squirrel's new hat?"
"Looks like he's trying too hard, that brat!"

Moss laughs softly, a cushion so plush,
While leaves wear stories in a hush.
Together they chuckle, soft and loud,
In this spot, they feel so proud.

So tiptoe close, but don't alarm,
These leafy friends, they mean no harm.
Join in the chatter, a plant-based chat,
Who knew greenery could be so sprat?

Secret Garden Symphony

In hidden nooks, where critters play,
The garden sings, hip-hip-hooray!
Flowers sway to a rhythmic tune,
Even worms have learned to croon.

Butterflies flutter, showcasing flair,
While daisies gossip, without a care.
The hedgehog hums a quiet beat,
As ants march on with their tiny feet.

Laughter bursts from blooming blooms,
Tickling the air with perfumed plumes.
A concert held beneath the sky,
With nature's creatures all nearby.

So grab a seat on zesty thyme,
And listen close, it's garden rhyme.
For every blossom, a note to share,
In this orchestra, fun fills the air.

Vibrant Shadows of Growth

In a patch of sun, where shadows play,
A tomato shimmies in a merry way.
Cucumbers curl in a giddy dance,
While sprouts are just dreaming of their chance.

The carrots whisper underground jokes,
Laughing at the little garden folks.
Radishes wear a rosy glow,
While peas in pods start their show.

Together they chuckle, roots intertwined,
A vibrant laughter, oh how they unwind.
Weeds chant verses, though often slight,
In this botanical, comedic night.

So sit down here, and take it in,
Join the laughter, let the fun begin.
For in this garden, wild and free,
Life's not just seeds, it's harmony!

Palette of Earth and Air

In pots where colors burst and swim,
A painter's dream hangs on a whim.
Petunias flaunt their flashy hues,
While daisies sport their polka dot views.

The sunflowers boast, they're tallest, no doubt,
While violets smirk, "We're cute, there's no rout."
Together they paint the canvas wild,
Nature's palette makes every heart smiled.

Breezes mix scents in a merry swirl,
As bees buzz by and the butterflies twirl.
"Get in line!" the spinach cheekily sings,
As blossoms chatter about royal things.

Underneath this vibrant spread,
Laughter bubbles between the bed.
In this artistry of flora and air,
Joy blooms bright, everywhere!

Essence of the Canopy

Under the leaves, I found a friend,
A squirrel in pajamas, what a trend!
He offered me nuts for a dance or two,
Now I'm a dancer in the forest crew.

We twirled with branches, laughed at the rain,
Both of us giggling, completely insane.
A pine tree giggled, 'Oh, look at them go!'
Nature's own circus, putting on a show.

Whispers of Wildflower Dreams

In a meadow bright, the daisies prance,
Winking at bees in a polka dot dance.
A butterfly landed, it tickled my nose,
I sneezed out a dandelion—had to compose!

The wind made me laugh, it whispered a joke,
About a sad tulip who couldn't invoke.
With petals a-flutter, and giggles galore,
Nature's the comedian we all can adore.

Rooms Alive with Green

In my fun-filled space, the plants like to speak,
Ferns tease each other, calling for a sneak.
"I'm taller!" one yells, while the others just shrug,
I chuckle and think: 'Oh, the tales they mug!'

A cactus chimed in, "I've got the best spikes!"
"Oh please!" said a fern, "I'm full of nice hikes!"
In this lively abode, nature's not shy,
My walls are alive with a giggle and sigh.

Shades of Renewal

Under the shade of the giggling trees,
A worm on a leaf has some brown bag cheese.
He shared with a snail, "This is top-class fare!"
The snail just replied, "No time for a share!"

Vines wrapped around me, they want to ensnare,
"Join our dance party, we all fit in here!"
I laughed with the leaves as they whispered my name,
In this lively patch, it's all just a game.

Lush Interlude

In a corner where the sun does shine,
Potted plants form a leafy line.
Frogs in hats dance without a care,
Sipping tea in the soothing air.

A cactus with a flashy grin,
Says it's a party, let's begin!
Silly snails with disco moves,
Groove beneath the leafy grooves.

Linen curtains gently sway,
As singing bugs come out to play.
A hamster dressed in shades of green,
Declares this space a lively scene.

In this merry patch of cheer,
Laughter echoes loud and clear.
With every bloom, the joy will bloom,
In this delightfully wild room.

Blooming Solitude

Alone, but not in silence so,
With a fern that steals the show.
It whispers jokes through leafy seams,
Turning solitude to silly dreams.

A flower prances, wearing crown,
While daisies tease with a soft frown.
The idle pot, a sage-like sage,
Makes puns that never quite age.

In this hallowed patch of green,
A rubber plant plays the queen.
With water droplets on its leaves,
It laughs at all the tricks it weaves.

As sunlight drizzles through the panes,
The laughter nearly drives me insane.
In this solitude so bizarre,
Every petal sparkles like a star.

Hideaway in Hues

Behind the door, a riot brews,
With pots and paints in vibrant hues.
A tulip wears a purple tie,
While daisies whirl as passersby.

The wallpaper is green as grass,
Where gnomes in boots all strut and sass.
They hold a meeting at noon's crest,
Declaring garden parties best.

A chameleon turns shades of cheese,
And giggles run with every breeze.
The orchids chat in rhyming verse,
Making the mundane seem diverse.

In this bright and zesty maze,
Even shadows dance with praise.
Laughter sprinkles through the air,
In this colorful affair.

Whispering Ferns

Whispers float from leafy hands,
As ferns gossip about plants' lands.
With comedic flair, a succulent grins,
Telling tales of watering sins.

The ivy's jokes are long and twist,
While every vine gives a hearty fist.
They poke fun at the potted rose,
Who's convinced it knows how to pose.

Laughter bounces off tiled floors,
As plants engage in playful wars.
With every chuckle, they expand,
Creating mischief, oh so grand!

From vibrant leaves, a chorus sings,
Celebrating all the joy that springs.
In this green retreat of gleeful turns,
Carefree life, oh how it yearns!

A Field of Possibilities

In fields where daisies dance and sway,
I lost my hat, it flew away!
A rabbit borrowed it for a while,
Now he hops with trendy style.

The sunbeams tickle, the grass is bright,
I twirl like a dancer, feeling light.
A blushing bee buzzes on by,
I swear it started to laugh and fly!

In this vast room of nature's play,
I tripped on roots, shouted hooray!
The sky winked down, cheeky and grand,
While squirrels judged my poor dance stand.

So here I lie, in petals spread,
With hats and rabbits swimming in my head.
In a realm where silly reigns supreme,
Life's just a patchwork, a feathered dream.

Adrift in Green Currents

I float on leaves, a giddy boat,
A frog's my captain, what a joke!
He croaks commands, I steer with flair,
Waving to ducks perched in midair.

The breeze is giggling, the trees are swaying,
While tiny bugs are out there playing.
I tried to do a backflip, but
Landed in moss, oh, a sticky rut!

The sun's a jokester, peeking through,
Tickling my nose, just like you do.
A cloud, it puffs with laughter loud,
As I twirl around, feeling quite proud.

So here I drift, no worries near,
With slimy pals and plenty of cheer.
This green adventure, a madcap spree,
Living my best life, wild and free.

Climbing Vines of Reflection

I climbed a vine, oh what a thrill,
Slipped on a leaf, down the hill!
The ground was soft, a cushy embrace,
Laughed with the flowers; what a race!

A parrot squawked, "Are you alright?"
I waved my arms, gave a silly fright.
It winked and said, "Just charm the crowd!"
So I danced amongst petals, feeling proud.

The sun was my spotlight, shining bright,
Bugs tapping feet to the rhythm of light.
I slid on the tendrils, feeling so spry,
Sang a ditty that made the leaves cry!

So when you climb where the green things grow,
Remember to giggle, steal the show.
In this sticky maze where joys entwine,
Life's just a climb on the vine of time.

The Sigh of Willow

Oh willow tree, with branches so long,
You sigh and you sway to a whimsical song.
I asked for advice, but you just drooped,
Giggled and whispered, "Life's just a loop!"

With each gentle rustle, the whispers flow,
Telling tales of winds that come and go.
I leaned closer, thought I might hear,
But the squirrels were chattering, loud and clear!

They crafted a nest in the crook of your arm,
Planning a wedding, what a charm!
I clapped my hands, said, "What a sight!"
The dance of the leaves, oh what delight!

So sigh your secrets, dear willow wise,
With roots in laughter, under summer skies.
In this golden hour, let humor bloom,
As we share our joys, in this leafy room.

The Breath of Moss

In a corner where critters play,
Moss invites them all for a stay.
Frogs sing their silly little tune,
While slugs moonwalk under the moon.

A squirrel held a dance party delight,
With acorns tossed, oh what a sight!
The grass laid down a carpet wide,
As twigs and leaves swayed side to side.

Enchanted Leafy Hideaway

In a hut of leaves, the fairies peek,
Mice play poker, oh what a freak!
Old tree trunks wear crowns of green,
With stories of mischief yet unseen.

A babbling brook boasts of its flow,
While whispering secrets we'd love to know.
Caterpillars count as they munch,
Zucchini dreams, over a crunchy lunch.

Emerald Retreat

Under the canopy, laughter roams,
Lizards gilt in shimmering tomes.
Dandelions crown the weary ants,
Who run in little wonky pants!

The whispers of wind, a giggly gale,
Ruffle the feathers of every snail.
In this oasis of verdant dreams,
Nothing is ever quite what it seems.

Nurtured by Nature

A cup of sunshine, a sprinkle of rain,
This garden's got the best of the gain.
Squirrels stash nuts like it's a crime,
Debating the meaning of 'just in time.'

With ladybugs keeping the gossip alive,
And butterflies causing a chaotic jive.
A plant with a grin and roots that dance,
In nature's embrace, all take a chance.

A Hidden Grove's Solace

In a nook where leaves just laugh,
Squirrels debate on the best path,
A gnome with cap sings a tune,
While shadows dance in bright afternoon.

The mushrooms wear tiny hats,
Critters gossip, sharing spats,
A frog on a log plays the drum,
As bees tap dance to the hum.

Joking vines wave 'hello',
While cuckoos put on a show,
The sun makes a warm, bright tease,
As worms wiggle with such ease.

In this grove, life's quite absurd,
Each chirping song, a bit of word,
With laughter bubbling all around,
Nature's jokes forever found.

Fern-Filled Embrace

In ferns that stretch and sway,
Lizards take naps all day,
A rabbit thinks he's quite regal,
While doing a jig on one leg, a beagle!

The leaves gossip in the breeze,
As flowers tickle with great tease,
A worm in a hat gives a bow,
To ants who raise eyebrows, wow!

The sun winks from behind a cloud,
As mushrooms wear coats, feeling proud,
A snail joins in a race, oh dear,
But ends up stuck, full of cheer.

With laughter hidden in each shade,
Every corner a joke is made,
In ferns where secrets whisper low,
Joy sprouts gently, don't you know?

Soliloquy of the Saplings

Young sprouts stand and speak with flair,
Confusing the beetles in their care,
One says, 'I feel like a tree!',
Another sighs, 'Just let me be!'

With winds that whip and twirl around,
Twigs high-five on the ground,
An acorn starts declaring, 'Hey!
I'm bound for greatness, hip-hip-hooray!'

Old branches chime in with a groan,
Sharing stories of seeds they've grown,
As shadows chuckle in delight,
While squirrels argue who's more bright.

In the heart of this vibrant jest,
Saplings strive to be their best,
A playful scene of growth unfolds,
As nature's humor gently molds.

Lush Corners of the Mind

In patches where daydreams bloom,
Thoughts collide and spin with zoom,
A chubby squirrel plans a feast,
While pondering if nuts taste least.

Greens swirl like a painter's brush,
And echoes chatter in a hush,
The grass tickles with a grin,
While daisies dance to a jaunty din.

Imaginations take a dive,
Where silliness is sure to thrive,
An idea takes flight like a bird,
With laughter trailing every word.

Here in this space of playful gleam,
Where trees wear thoughts like a dream,
Joyously lost in verdant sway,
Turning whims into a bouquet.

Canvas of the Foresthesis

In a room where trees wear hats,
And squirrels throw wild dance spats.
Cacti sip tea while they play chess,
This place is pure nature's mess.

Moss carpets the floor like a rug,
While vines give each other a hug.
Bubbles of laughter float in the air,
Who knew nature could be so rare?

There's a frog who thinks he can sing,
He croaks out tunes as if he's a king.
The flowers all giggle and sway,
As they join in the vibrant ballet.

And as the sun sets with a grin,
The fireflies come out to spin.
In this forest, oh what a sight!
Even the shadows dance with delight.

Lush Abode of Imagination

A room where clouds sit on a chair,
And pine trees toss their scented hair.
The raccoons wear ties and debate,
About snacks and their favorite fate.

Gnomes in a line wait for soup,
While ladybugs form a dance troop.
Amidst daisies brimming with glee,
Everyone's too happy to flee.

Fluffy rabbits munch on some cheese,
While owls share jokes that bring a tease.
A snail races against a leaf,
Leaving all the critters in disbelief.

In a nook where whimsy runs wild,
Every creature feels like a child.
With laughter echoing through the trees,
It's a place that can only please.

Bounty of Blossoms

In a garden where daisies wear crowns,
The butterflies pull silly pranks in towns.
Sunbeams play tag with the morning dew,
While petals whisper secrets anew.

Tulips gossip about their best dress,
While daisies hold a flower press.
The bees are the judges of sweet tunes,
As they buzz to rhythm under the moons.

A cat with a monocle sips tea,
While a dog tries to climb up a tree.
They chuckle and brush off the dirt,
In this place, who cares about hurt?

When the night falls with a yawn,
Stars join in, beginning to dawn.
Dreams sprout wings, take flight in glee,
As blossoms laugh under the tree.

Numberless Leaves of Peace

Among the leaves, there's giggles of light,
As shadows tease everyone in sight.
The owl tells tales with a wink,
While squirrels sip cocoa and think.

There's a party in every bough,
With conga lines forming somehow.
Choruses of chirps fill the night,
As crickets join in, what a sight!

Rabbits wear party hats, it's true,
With balloons made of colorful dew.
A turtle does limbo under a leaf,
Filling the world with joy and belief.

At the end of the day, they all cheer,
Sharing laughter, spreading good cheer.
In this leafy wonder, find your bliss,
A forest of fun is hard to miss.

Allure of the Canopied Ceiling

Beneath the leaves, a sight so grand,
Laughter echoes, with a helping hand.
A squirrel swings, with style and grace,
While I'm just tripping over my shoelace.

I pour my tea, but it's met with a leak,
Nature's giggles are all that I seek.
A flower sneezes, how terribly rude!
Here I sit, in vibrant mood.

I'd hang up a banner of bright, bold green,
But know too well, my room's never clean.
With vines overhead, a chaotic sight,
Who needs a beach when you've got this delight?

The ceiling's a jungle, the jokes are lush,
Amidst the ferns, I'm in quite the rush.
Yet here I thrive in this leafy haze,
Laughing at life in all its maze!

Canopy Conversations

Under the tent of tangled vines,
A chattering bug spins its witty lines.
It claims to know the gossip of trees,
While I sip my drink with a clumsy sneeze.

"Hey there, flower!" I call with glee,
"Why do you bloom? For a party or me?"
The petals shrug in playful jest,
"Just trying to impress the buzzing guest."

With every chirp, the banter grows,
A mushroom chimes in, "You're stepping on toes!"
The leaf-laden crowd gets rowdy and loud,
As I ponder my place in this leafy crowd.

And time slips by like a vine on the wall,
In this verdant haven, we're having a ball.
With every giggle, the colors cheer,
Nature's punchlines ring, oh so clear!

Unraveled in Green Comfort

Wrapped in leaves, so snug and neat,
I wear a crown of daisies at my feet.
A snail slides by with a wink and grin,
"Looks like you're losing! Where do I begin?"

The cushions here are made of moss,
I take a breather, relaxing like a boss.
A wise old toad croaks, "Join my book club!"
But I can't concentrate, I'm stuck in the scrub.

With every laugh, the shadows dance,
While I yell at the roaches, "You missed your chance!"
A game of hide and seek with a bee,
I'm scrumptious repast, but I'm still feeling free.

So here I am, in this leafy delight,
Where comfort abounds and giggles take flight.
Unraveled and wild, I find my sweet home,
In this jovial realm, I'm free to roam!

Reverberation of Verdancy

In echoing greens, the laughter rings,
As I juggle ferns like circus things.
The vines all tease, with sly, little grins,
"Careful now, watch out for those spins!"

The shadows plot, and branches sway,
While I declare, "Let's play charades today!"
A flower raises a petal for guess,
"Is it a garden?" I must confess.

My dancing leaves drop down in glee,
As I prance around, enthusiastic and free.
The winks of daisies add charm to the scene,
In this comedy show of tasteful green.

With giggles galore, the breezes do shift,
A playful breeze gives my costume a lift.
Amidst the cackles, I twirl in the space,
Reverberating joy in this floral embrace!

Sanctuary of Verdure

In the corner, a cactus wears a hat,
A rubber plant dances, how about that?
The fern is gossiping with the shy peace lily,
While the spider plant tries to look oh-so-chilly.

The pothos climbs, reaching for the light,
Knocking over cups in a clumsy delight.
The daisies giggle as they sway left and right,
While the snake plant snickers, feeling quite bright.

In this green world, we laugh and we play,
Finding joy in the leaves, come what may.
With soil on our shoes, we'll dance like a fool,
Because who needs rules when plants make the cool?

So let's toast with some water, a shrub's finest drink,
Raise a glass to the blooms, let our spirits not sink.
In this quirky realm, where green things do bloom,
We're all a bit silly in our verdant room.

Sanctuary Beyond the Window

Outside the glass, the squirrels all play,
While we chuckle at their clumsy ballet.
A sunflower winks, showing off its big grin,
As I try to ignore the dust bunnies' din.

The hummingbird zooms, a green little jet,
Mistaking my hair for a flower pet.
Leaves whisper secrets, in wind's gentle tease,
While I sip my tea under the shade of the trees.

The daisies gossip, their petals a-matter,
Chatting about how the rabbits are fatter.
While the ivy creeps slowly up the wall,
Trying to eavesdrop on all that we call.

Let's throw on our hats and join nature's parade,
Embrace every chuckle, let worries cascade.
With flora and fauna, our spirits take flight,
In this joyous domain, everything feels right.

A Tapestry of Leaves

Leaves of emerald, weave a tale that's absurd,
Whispering secrets that are best left unheard.
Snapping at sunlight, they play peek-a-boo,
Taking bets on how many clouds will pass through.

A chubby little beetle rolls by with a grin,
Proclaiming his kingdom, declaring he'll win!
The mushrooms plot mischief beneath the old oak,
While crickets compose, strumming tunes like a folk.

With petals like confetti, we toss them around,
Creating a spectacle, joy's finally found.
A toad hops in rhythm, a dancer in glee,
While the flowers assess who's the best VIP.

So let us embrace this botanical glee,
With laughter as bright as a buzzing bumblebee.
In a world full of green, let's drummer our cheer,
Because nature's a party, the vibe's always near.

Tranquil Oasis Within

In a cozy nook, where the plants are aglow,
A rubber tree sways, putting on quite a show.
The creeping thyme plots its next little trip,
While the potted herbs gossip over a sip.

The geraniums cackle, discussing their bloom,
While my cat inspects every nook of the room.
With fronds like fanfare, they dance in delight,
Creating a chorus that feels just right.

"Who is the funniest?" asks gentle jade,
While mocking the orchids in a sly masquerade.
The ivy rolls its eyes at the cacti so proud,
Sharing inside jokes, laughing out loud.

Let us join the ruckus, weave laughter in air,
For in this green kingdom, there's joy everywhere.
With a wink and a nudge, let the laughter resume,
In our quirky oasis, where fun's always in bloom!

Chamber of Rejuvenation

In a space full of green, it's a wild dream,
The plants giggle softly, like a springtime theme.
I tried to meditate, found a snail in my shoe,
He waved as he passed, said, 'Hey, what's new?'

The ferns do a dance, with leaves all a-flutter,
While a chubby toad croaks, 'What's all this clutter?'
I pour out my woes, but they just sprout wings,
They laugh as they fly and dance on springs.

Mirthful Murmurs of the Grove

In a grove filled with laughter, the trees tell their tales,
Of squirrels with acorns, and tea parties with snails.
A chipmunk in bowtie serves cookies with charm,
And a raccoon serenades with an accordion's balm.

The mushrooms throw parties, all dressed to the nines,
With fungi confetti and swampy divines.
They boogie through dusk with a jiggly beat,
These woodland folks know how to groove on their feet.

Verdant Reverie

In a dream where the leaves play tricks on the mind,
Laughter echoes loudly, it's chaos combined.
A cactus tells jokes that make others groan,
While a daisy named Daisy starts to bemoan.

Each corner's a party, each shadow a friend,
As vines twist together, they happily blend.
The happiness rises like bubbles in soap,
I grin at the madness, with glee in its scope.

Blossoms of Solitude

In solitude's garden, where humor is spry,
A daffodil snickers as bees buzz on by.
Alone, but not lonely, the clovers all grin,
A pot-bellied gnome pours tea with a spin.

The petals all gossip, with secrets to share,
While the wind gives a nudge, to ruffle my hair.
I laugh at the thoughts that bloom with delight,
In this wild little world, everything's just right.

Wild Flora Embrace

In a patch of daisies, I find my way,
Waving at bees who just want to play.
A sunflower winks, it's got jokes to tell,
While dandelions plot to cast magic spells.

With vines like siblings, they tease and tug,
Twisting and turning—oh, what a shrug!
Each leaf has a tickle, a laugh, a cheer,
Nature's own frolic, so bright and clear.

Red berries giggle, they bounce with glee,
A berry punch party, come join, yippee!
Moss hugs the ground, a carpet of fun,
In this wild embrace, there's room for everyone.

So come take a stroll in this leafy delight,
Where the laughter of petals makes everything bright.
Forget your worries, let nature consume,
In this lush little haven, there's always more room.

Sanctuary in Shade

Underneath broad branches, all laughter's free,
Caterpillars cha-cha—just wait 'til they're bees!
A light breeze whispers, 'Let's pull up a chair,'
While squirrels debate who's the king of this lair.

Frogs in a chorus sing croaks of delight,
Trying to outhop each other in spite.
The coolness of shadows, a playful embrace,
In this sanctuary, let's quicken the pace!

The sun peek-a-boos through leaves like a kid,
Shining on flowers that dance—oh, what a bid!
A gopher pops up with a grin of pure bliss,
Attracting the attention of a curious kiss.

Come join the hilarity under this shade,
Life's but a joke, and we've got it made.
In laughter and joy, let's whimsically blend,
In this cool hideaway, the fun never ends.

Botanical Dreams Unfurled

In pots lined in rows, where the mischief grows,
Cacti wear hats—bit prickly, I suppose.
A geranium snickers, a plant pot affair,
With ivy and ferns doing daring hair.

With petals like pages from fairy tale books,
They gossip and giggle, giving sly looks.
On shelves they conspire, a stemmed conspiracy,
A bloom's true desire—a garden spree!

Sweet peas play tag in the sunlight's warm glow,
Racing and chasing, just putting on a show.
While rosemary shares some snarky remarks,
Encouraging mischief in dainty green parks.

So welcome this banter of blossoms that tease,
In botanical dreams where we do as we please.
Let's water the laughter and watch it take flight,
In a world full of color, everything's right.

Cypress Embrace

Among tall sentinels, where the laughter rings,
Squirrels exchange secrets, discussing their flings.
Rooted together, they sway side to side,
In a trunk-to-trunk hug, the cypress won't hide.

With a whispering breeze and a chuckle in tow,
Leaves tickle the branches, putting on quite a show.
Pinecones drop down with a clatter, a clunk,
And giggly old owls chirp tales from the trunk.

They huddle in shadows, beneath the tall trees,
Negotiating sunbaths with rustling leaves.
Their bark is all laughter, no wood-like despair,
In this whimsical grove, we play without care.

So join the green gathering, the fun is profound,
In this cypress embrace, magic's all around.
From roots to the sky, let joy intertwine,
In life's merry jests, everything will align.

Embers of Spring

In a corner where the plant pots dance,
The spider plant sways with a chance.
A cactus grins, it's prickly yet bright,
It cracks jokes in the middle of night.

A fern unfurls with a theatrical flair,
While daisies gossip without a care.
The air is thick with laughter and cheer,
Each leaf nods wisely, "No worries here!"

As raindrops tap the windowpanes,
The soil giggles, sharing its gains.
A beetle recites a comedic play,
"Why did the flower get stuck in ballet?"

Amidst the cheer of each leafy plume,
They toast with tea in this cozy room.
With colorful pots and whims galore,
Spring's silliness reigns forevermore.

Haven of Harmony

In a nook where the sunshine beams bright,
A potbellied plant declares it's alright.
The chubby old fern with a wiggly leaf,
Has the best jokes, beyond all belief.

A row of succulents wears shady hats,
They chuckle softly like cheeky old cats.
The air carries hints of sweet minty fun,
As rosemary twirls under the sun.

While ivy climbs with a smile that's sly,
It whispers secrets like "How high can you fly?"
A cricket nearby starts to tap dance,
With beats that inspire, it's quite a romance!

And as twilight peeks in through the leaves,
They sip berry tea, sharing old heaves.
In this haven filled with giggles galore,
They find joy in nature, forevermore.

Lush Whispers of Nature

Among the ferns, there's a charismatic sage,
Telling tales of its greener age.
A sunflower winks with a sassy remark,
"Do you think I'm brighter than the spark?"

Down on the floor, the moss takes a nap,
Dreaming of flowers and a giant map.
While petals scatter, with laughs, they fly,
"Who needs a cloud if you can just sigh?"

A ladybug spins with a giggly glee,
Joking 'round as it hops from tree to tree.
The daisies are plotting a stand-up show,
"Why did the flower never take it slow?"

With todbuds stirring adventurous dreams,
Their laughter rejoices in playful themes.
Together they bloom in this frolicsome land,
Nature's humor forever grand.

Emerald Echoes

In a patch where colors collide and flare,
A leafy comedian has stories to share.
The hosta cracks up at its own silly pose,
While tulips laugh, waving fancy pink toes.

The moss giggles softly, a plush little seat,
"Why are plants so good at hiding their heat?"
As vines twist and turn in a breezy display,
Chasing shadows in a rambunctious ballet.

A frog joins in with a croaky delight,
"Why did I leap in the middle of night?"
The petals all roar, roll around in pure glee,
"Stop, you're making it hard to see!"

As the day fades, and stars twinkle bright,
The emerald crew giggles, what a sight!
In their emerald world, the laughter won't stop,
Nature's cheeky comedy—always on top.

Where Nature Sleeps

In a cozy nook where squirrels sigh,
Frogs wear ties as crickets fly.
The daisies giggle, the daisies bloom,
While ants throw parties in the gloom.

A hedgehog sneezes, it's quite a show,
The winds whisper secrets, but only they know.
A snail in slippers, moving quite slow,
Writes poems about friends he'll never outgrow.

Underneath trees that dance with glee,
A butterfly lands, drinks tea with a bee.
Rabbits in hats, juggling with flair,
As mushrooms tap-dance, without a care.

So many giggles where silence might spread,
With ticklish ferns poking about the head.
Beneath leaves where antics hold tight,
Nature's got jokes, oh what a sight!

Rustic Serenity

In a wooden chair, 'neath the starry skies,
A goat reads gossip with big, bulging eyes.
Chickens debate on who's the best lay,
While old man cactus naps through the day.

Pigs in pajamas trot on the lawn,
While vines whisper secrets from dusk until dawn.
A cat with a monocle sips on its stew,
As the vegetables gossip, spreading their view.

A jolly old fox brings pies to the fair,
Where ducks in tuxedos strut with rare flair.
Beneath twinkling lights made of fireflies bright,
The dances of dusk turn up the delight.

Oh, what a hoot! It's barnyard ballet,
With chickens on stage, all swaying away.
The sheep in the back knit sweaters with pride,
As laughter ignites in the countryside!

Sheltered in Foliage

Leafy umbrellas hang from the trees,
While berries plot mischief over the breeze.
A raccoon in disguise says 'You're looking fab,'
As chipmunks drink smoothies from a leafy slab.

Frogs in a band croaking riotous tunes,
Dancing with fireflies beneath the bright moons.
A rustle in bushes brings giggles and jumps,
As hedgehogs in sneakers bounce off the lumps.

Under the shelter, the laughter abounds,
With rabbits in roller skates spinning around.
The ants launch a rocket made out of clay,
And turn snack time into a glorious play.

So here in this patch of green whimsy and cheer,
Nature's committee gathers every year.
With each rustle and chuckle, let's give it a cheer,
For this silly slice of the world we hold dear!

Glade of Dreams

In a shimmering glade, where the giggles run free,
The daisies are plotting a grand jamboree.
Fireflies twirl in their sparkling outfits,
While mushrooms gossip about the best bits.

A moose brushes up on his boogie and sway,
While turtles play chess in a casual way.
A parade of critters, all dressed for the night,
Serve cake made of acorns, a wondrous sight.

The ivy's providing its silk for a stage,
As raccoons recite from a fairy tale page.
Squirrels sell tickets, don't lose your cash,
Or you'll find your snacks disappear in a flash!

So join in the fun, it's a wacky delight,
As laughter spills out, from morning till night.
In this magical place, with shenanigans brimmed,
Who would have thought that the woodland could be so whimsied?

Exchange of Colors and Breath

In this space where hues collide,
The walls wear shades they cannot hide.
A purple couch, a yellow chair,
I trip on colors everywhere!

A vibrant rug that tickles toes,
A ceiling painted like a rose.
Cushions gossip, patterns collide,
In this playful place, joy can't hide.

A chandelier made out of fruit,
Hangs above where funny vines shoot.
Bananas giggle, oranges dance,
In this room, chaos takes a chance!

With laughter bouncing off the walls,
Here? No one ever fears their falls.
We laugh so hard we might just roll,
In this room—colorful as a bowl!

Garden of Burgeoning Thoughts

Among the petals bright and bold,
Ideas sprout like marigolds.
A silly notion took its flight,
It bloomed and laughed in pure delight.

With daisies dancing in the breeze,
Thoughts mingle somewhat like the bees.
A ticklish breeze makes wisdom sway,
As thoughts and blooms begin to play.

A sunflower whispers, take a seat,
While lavender gives a fragrant treat.
In this curious plant-filled plot,
New perspectives grow on every spot.

So wander here, where minds expand,
And every seed of joy is planned.
With laughter sprouting like a vine,
In this garden, all is divine!

Ascent Among the Green

On this ladder made of leaves,
I climb where laughter never eaves.
Each step is squishy, oh so fun,
I slip and slide—who needs the sun?

A parrot shouts, "Don't look down!"
As I reach heights, it spins around.
With branches swaying, I lift my foot,
Then land right in a patch of fruit!

The breeze brings jokes from trees above,
A funny tune, the songs we love.
With giggles echoing far and wide,
In this green ascent, we take our ride.

So let's climb high and stretch our dreams,
In this green realm, nothing's as it seems.
With every tumble, laugh, and cheer,
The heights of fun are always near!

Meeting with the Verdant Spirits

In the forest where the colors sing,
I meet the sprites with leafy bling.
They giggle as I trip on roots,
And play hopscotch with the fruits.

A sprite declares, "I'm feeling blue!"
While another pops up, "I'm green too!"
They tickle ferns and tease the moss,
In this wild world, no one's the boss.

A jumpy toad joins in the fun,
Making puns in the afternoon sun.
With laughter that floats through the air,
Here, even branches dance with flair!

So join the spirits, take their hand,
In this giggly, green-expanding land.
Where jokes grow wild, and joy takes flight,
We'll laugh until it turns to night!

Petals Whispering Secrets

In a corner, blooms were gabbing,
Petals giggled, flowers flabbing.
A tulip whispered, 'Hey, what's new?'
The daisy replied, 'Just more sun, boo!'

Leaves were eavesdropping on blooms,
Sharing tales of garden looms.
'Did you hear about the rogue bee?'
'The one who thought he could climb a tree!'

Bees buzzing like they owned the plot,
Dandelions laughing, 'Ain't it hot?'
A cactus joked, 'What's the buzz today?'
While vines played hopscotch in the clay.

In this riot of colors bright,
Nature's laughter brought delight.
So if you wander near the patch,
You might just hear the flowers hatch!

Room Full of Life

A place where plants throw wild soirées,
Sipping sunlight in leafy bays.
Fern flirted with a bright marigold,
While succulents shared stories, bold.

Spider plants tapping their green toes,
Poches rolled over, striking poses.
'Have you heard the tale of the rose?'
'Oh please, she prunes her own nose!'

Fluttering butterflies showed up late,
Caught in the web of a spider's fate.
'Next time, prompt us with a hint,'
Said a rose, with a smug little print.

In this chamber, they have no care,
Just silly dances and a wild flair.
Grow a little joy, share a laugh,
In this room with nature's staff!

Cloistered in Nature's Grasp

Huddled plants in a cozy nook,
Chortled softly, reading a book.
A vine exclaimed, 'Can you believe?'
The flower grinned, 'I'd best not leave!'

Shrubs discussing the weather's tease,
While herbs debated on fairer leaves.
'What's hotter than this summer heat?'
Cactus snapped, 'Some spicy beet!'

Frogs croaking songs in every tone,
Polka-dot leaves laid down their own.
'These melodies are simply grand!'
A ladybug danced with a steady hand.

This cloistered chaos, a funny play,
Plants in their corner, come what may.
Join their laughter, come take a seat,
In this sanctuary, life is sweet!

Raindrops on Leafy Desires

Pitter-patter on the greens they go,
Raindrops giggling, putting on a show.
'Oh joy!' said the ferns, 'Let's dance in droplets!'
While daisies sang, 'We're in for some profits!'

Leaves splashing like kids in the sun,
Watering dreams, oh, what fun!
A rhododendron winked in the spray,
'Can't wait for the rainbow to play!'

Guided by whims of the breezy gusts,
Moss chuckled softly, 'In nature, we trust.'
A raindrop twirled, taking center stage,
As flowers giggled, defying age.

With smiles abound in this leafy raid,
Every drop a giggle, finely made.
Join the revelry, lose all your fears,
This is the kingdom nourished by cheers!

Verdant Whispers

In a nook where plants play peek-a-boo,
Laughter blooms in shades of green hue.
Thirsty ferns gossip, oh what a sight,
While cacti roll jokes, spiking the night.

A spider plant spins tales of the past,
As rubber trees dance, having a blast.
Pothos are plotting to steal the show,
While peace lilies laugh, 'We're the pros, you know!'

The air is thick with whimsical cheer,
Each leaf has a secret it whispers near.
Silly vines swing with no hint of gloom,
In this jolly patch, there's always room.

So come join the fun, leave worries behind,
In this lively spot where laughter is blind.
Every petal and sprout has a story to share,
In this jungle of joy, you'll find love everywhere.

Sanctuary of Leaves

There's a haven where laughter tickles the air,
With leafy companions who simply don't care.
Bamboo's mischief will make you just grin,
As they conspire, let the giggles begin.

The flowers are wearing their finest attire,
In this leafy realm, everyone's a flyer.
Vines twist around, sharing corny old jokes,
As daisies roll eyes at the punny old folks.

Silly seedlings stretch, bending with glee,
Wishing for sunlight, as bright as can be.
But shade-loving buddies just whisper and lol,
While asking, "Hey, who's putting up the wall?"

Come on down to this leafy delight,
Where greens share a laugh beneath soft moonlight.
This sanctuary of fun, oh what a sight,
With plants telling jokes, life feels so light!

Emerald Echoes

Here echoes the laugh of a jungly surprise,
Where yuccas and ferns plot the ultimate rise.
Each leaf has a punchline, a quirky old jest,
In this vibrant venue, it's hard to find rest.

Basil tickles senses, as mint joins the fray,
While hanging' in laughter keeps worries at bay.
A mock cactus quips, "I'm prickly, but cool,"
While an ivy retorts, "Hey, it's nature's rule!"

The color of joy shades the walls all around,
With emeralds dancing on the playful ground.
Every petal's a joker, a light-hearted flare,
In this space of green giggles—who could compare?

So swing on a vine, let your worries be few,
Join this garden of laughter, let laughter ensue.
In emerald echoes, the fun knows no limits,
As the plants throw a bash, you find yourself in it!

Room of Endless Growth

In a space where flora takes whimsy in flight,
Harvesting laughter from morning to night.
With each creeping vine, a new tale unfolds,
As ferns whisper secrets and poke at the mold.

The air is alive with hilarious cheer,
Wandering blooms nudge each other, "Come near!"
Sage gives a wink, "I'm the wisest around,"
While snapdragons snap at the jokes they have found.

Zinnias twirl as they dance with delight,
Decked out in zesty patterns, what a sight!
The potted greens giggle, sharing a tune,
As the sunlight smiles, "Dance away, my goons!"

So step into this mirth-filled grove of surprise,
Where giggles grow wild like the stars in the skies.
In this room bursting forth with laughter and bloom,
You'll find endless growth, and joy will consume!

Nestled in Green

In a chair made of leaves, I sit tight,
Sipping tea brewed from sunlight bright.
The curtains are vines, the floor's a soft bed,
With a squirrel as my butler, he offers me bread.

My neighbor's a frog, he croaks a salute,
Wears a top hat made of a gnarled old root.
He tells me the gossip, what's hot in the wood,
And offers me crumpets, though they're mostly just 'food'.

The flowers all giggle, their petals so wide,
They play peek-a-boo, with bees by their side.
The sun's got a grin, it's shining like new,
As I dance with the daisies, wearing grass for a shoe!

In this room of enchantment, with laughter galore,
Where the grass grows a carpet right up to the door.
I've invited a fox for a wild party spree,
He brought his best moves—let's just say, I'm tea!

Secrets of the Canopy

Up high in the trees, where the squirrels all play,
Secrets hang heavy, like leaves in the fray.
A parrot's my spy, with tales of delight,
He squawks out the drama from morning to night.

I found a lost acorn, it whispered to me,
Said it was waiting for its own tree spree.
With giggles, it rolled, and I couldn't resist,
The notion that acorns can have quite the twist.

The branches are crowded with critters in hats,
A raccoon in a tux, and the birds, they wear bats!
Each branch is a room, a new party to crash,
Where laughter abounds and the pinecones all splash.

In this leafy lounge, we're all guests of the woods,
Playing hide and seek in the neighborly hoods.
The breeze sings a tune, a hilarious rhyme,
As we dance on the branches, we're having a time!

The Realm of Moss

On a throne made of moss, I recline with flair,
The mushrooms all gossip, not a worry or care.
They tell me of fairies, who sneak bread at night,
With crumbs that are sparkling, oh what a sight!

The walls cry with laughter, they're covered in green,
Each moss-covered stone has a grin, so serene.
I chuckle with puddles, they ripple with joy,
Together we plot, like a mischievous ploy.

A chipmunk in stripes sings the latest news,
With his ruffled-up feathers, he can't help but cruise.
In my room of soft cushions, we dance with delight,
While the beetles are drumming on through the night.

So here in this place where the whimsy is great,
I'll invite all my friends for a mossy debate.
As we giggle and roll in the emerald bed,
With secrets from nature filling our head!

Forest's Heart

In the heart of the woods, where the wild things dwell,
I found a great fortune, a moss-covered shell.
It whispered of joy, in a voice oh so sly,
And promised me laughter, if just I'd comply.

With the trees as my friends, we laughed till we cried,
The trunks doubled over, we couldn't decide.
Should we sway with the breeze, or sing to the sky?
Every rustle a punchline, oh me, oh my!

A woodpecker's drumming forms beats we can groove,
And the flowers all sway, with a jazzy old move.
In this heart of the forest, I reign as the queen,
With sage advice from a turtle, who's never seen green!

So come join my party where the wild creatures play,
We'll feast on the laughter, till night turns to day.
In this realm where we giggle, let worries take flight,
In the heart of the woods, everything's alright!

Palette of Petals

In a garden of quirky blooms,
The daisies gossip, share their tunes.
With sun hats on, they sway and sway,
As tulips giggle the day away.

A dandelion wears a crown of gold,
While roses blush, their tales unfold.
The bees come buzzing, they love the scene,
A party of petals, bright and keen.

Oh, if the weeds could only dance,
They'd fashion rhymes and take a chance.
But stuck in soil, they fume and stew,
Their lack of flair is quite the boo-hoo!

Let's sip some nectar, toast to cheer,
Amidst the colors, laughter's near.
A palette of petals, vibrant and bold,
In this funny space, no secrets told.

Comfort in Chlorophyll

In the shade of leaves so lush and wide,
A squirrel named Larry takes a ride.
He tries to nap on a branch so small,
But bounces off, oh dear, what a fall!

Fern fronds chuckle, watching the spree,
While daisies debate if they too can be.
A merry band of flora in bloom,
Providing comfort, erasing gloom.

The moss is soft, a green velvet bed,
Where beetles play chess with crumbs of bread.
They raise their stakes, a sport so grand,
In our leafy haven, nature's band.

So come and join this leafy cheer,
In chlorophyll comfort, spread the good cheer.
With laughter and frolic, we'll surely stay,
In this quirky space of green and play!

Space of Growth and Glow

In a pot so small, a cactus dreams,
Of grand adventures with sunbeam teams.
He wiggles his spines, a quirky sight,
While daisies roll their eyes with delight.

A pair of socks lost in the yard,
Whispering secrets, oh my, how bizarre!
The ivy creeps up for a peek or two,
While petunias gossip, and all is askew.

In this space where nonsense can thrive,
Every sprout seems perfectly alive.
The sun winks down, casting playful light,
On this funny scene, everything feels right.

Let's dance like blades of grass in the breeze,
A merry jig among the trees.
In our garden of jest, let laughter flow,
In this cozy nook where we all can grow.

Aurora's Grassy Lounge

In Aurora's lounge, the grass does chat,
With floppy hats and a big old mat.
A turtle sips his herbal tea,
While bugs play chess, oh what glee!

The daisies lay back, their petals splayed,
While ants play music in a leafy glade.
With laughter they tumble, a comical sight,
In this cozy nook, where all feels right.

A mischievous breeze fluffs up their attire,
As butterflies dance, their wings on fire.
It's a lounge of fun, with silliness rife,
Where nature and laughter come together in life.

So come find your spot on this emerald stage,
Join the jests of the grass, let's turn the page.
In Aurora's space of merry delight,
We'll laugh with the flora from morning till night.

The Verdant Embrace

In a jungle of socks, they play hide and seek,
A cactus in slippers gives out quite a squeak.
The fern wears a hat, quite tall and stout,
Laughing at shadows that dance all about.

A rubbery plant keeps time with a tick,
While others just giggle at a broom's little trick.
The vines tell the jokes while the orchids just sway,
In this leafy abode, who needs a café?

A snail on a skateboard zips round and round,
As the tree roots tap-dance, oh what a sound!
In the corner, a toad has a tea party spree,
With fig newtons and cookies, just wait and see!

So if you're feeling down, come join in the fun,
With giggly green pals, your worries will run.
A jungle of laughter, it's all by design,
In this colorful nook, everything's fine!

Palette of Pines

A pinecone's a painter with a brush made of thyme,
Mixing colors of laughter, creating pure rhyme.
The sap's like glue, holding giggles in place,
While squirrels share secrets with a squeaky embrace.

Here comes a raccoon, wearing glasses for style,
Counting the stars and cracking a smile.
Moss wears a tutu, ready to dance,
While the sunbeams cheer in a playful romance.

The branches hold parties for bugs in a line,
With disco balls twirling, it's simply divine.
A caterpillar DJ spins tunes oh so bright,
As the flowers keep swaying, what a beautiful sight!

So if you're in need of a chuckle or cheer,
Join the pine paint party, your worries won't rear.
With each leafy brushstroke, the laughter's assured,
In this vibrant chaos, you'll feel so adored!

Leafy Reverie

There's a banana by day, a plantain by night,
Telling tall tales with pure delight.
A pot full of noodles grows roots with a grin,
While radishes giggle at the mess they're in.

The sunflowers gossip about last week's grand ball,
While peas and beans have a springtime brawl.
The sprouts on the windowsill dance in a line,
As the air filled with giggles feels simply divine.

The beans play the banjo, the carrots do tap,
While lettuce in leg warmers embraces the flap.
And through all this chaos, just one thing is clear,
This leafy abode brings pure joy and good cheer!

So borrow a fork and a spoon from the shelf,
Join in the fun, be a wee leafy elf.
With flowers for hats and a bowl made of thyme,
In this silly sanctuary, it's laughter time!

Beyond the Window

Outside the pane where the garden can play,
A gnome hops along, brightening the day.
With a hat that's too big and shoes with a squeak,
He dances with daisies, it's joy that they seek.

The ladybugs clap, they can't keep from grinning,
As the roses tell stories about summer beginning.
A cabbage in sneakers jogs by with a tune,
While the tulips sip tea under the light of the moon.

In a world full of whimsy, adventures are near,
Where laughter is sprouted, and worries disappear.
Each breeze brings a chuckle, each raindrop a song,
In this vibrant domain, you'll feel you belong.

So peek through the window, don't stay stuck inside,
Join all of the fun, let your heart be your guide.
With colors and giggles, let your spirit roam,
In a garden that welcomes you home, sweet home!

Under a Canopy of Calm

Beneath a roof of leafy cheer,
Squirrels dance, not a worry near.
A pigeon struts with swagger proud,
While ants form parades, a tiny crowd.

Laughter echoes in the breeze,
As bees wear hats atop the trees.
A rabbit hops, it tells a joke,
And playfully teases a nearby oak.

The sun peeks through with a cheeky grin,
While frogs croak songs to the buzzing din.
A gopher waves from the lush green mound,
Where silliness and joy abound.

With every rustle, a giggle shared,
In this corner, no one is scared.
A hammock swings, where dreams take flight,
In a realm of laughter, pure delight.

The Nest of Nature's Palette

A canvas bright above our heads,
Where colors play on nature's beds.
The flowers bloom with giggles sweet,
While snails have races on the street.

A painter bird dips in the hive,
Creating swirls, oh, how they thrive!
The grass giggles as we sit down,
A lively art show on the ground.

Umbrella mushrooms sprout with flair,
Each one a hat, for those who dare.
The ladybugs dress in red and dots,
Hosting wild tea parties in various spots.

The sun splashes gold on every leaf,
While crickets harmonize in brief.
In this nest of joy and cheer,
Laughter dances through the year.

Hues of Harmony

Colors clash in a playful fight,
With violets sneaking up at night.
Yellows giggle, the reds roll by,
While greens conspiring with a sly eye.

The leaves erupt like popcorn's pop,
As nature's brushes happily swap.
A rainbow spills down from blue,
As puddles splash with every hue.

Dandelions wear their poofy crowns,
While critters prance in tiny towns.
With each unique shade, they all agree,
Life's a party, come watch and see!

In this vibrant world of glee,
Where laughs are free, as they should be.
Together we swirl in our playful spree,
Dancing with nature, just let it be!

Forest's Caress

A ticklish breeze through branches flows,
While giggling leaves put on their shows.
The squirrels chat with a wink and nod,
As wildflowers play tag with the sod.

Mushrooms sprout like unexpected guests,
As the animals plan their silly quests.
A bear waltzes with a swaying tree,
While wise old owls sip herbal tea.

The sun peeks in with a blushing smile,
Tickling grass for a little while.
A path of giggles beneath our feet,
Where every step presents a treat.

In this embrace of wild delight,
Every creature finds their light.
With laughter ringing all around,
In nature's arms, joy knows no bound.

www.ingramcontent.com/pod-product-compliance
Lightning Source LLC
Chambersburg PA
CBHW072215070526
44585CB00015B/1342